IN YOUR WILDEST DREAMS

Imagination at Work

Cover Artist

Cathy Saksa lives in New York City and Long Beach Island, New Jersey, with her husband. She makes collages and cut-paper illustrations—types of art that are made by cutting out pictures or shapes and pasting them on a background. The cover of this book is an example of a photo collage.

ISBN 0-673-80036-9

Acknowledgments appear on page 128.

12345678910 VHJ 9998979695949392

IN YOUR WILDEST DREAMS

Imagination at Work

■ ScottForesman

A Division of HarperCollinsPublishers

CONTENTS

I Can Do That!
Genre Study

That's Entertainment from Bill Peet!
Author Study

No Problem!

Student Resources

RAGTIME TUMPIE

WRITTEN BY

ALAN SCHROEDER

PAINTINGS BY

BERNIE FUCHS

Each morning, before the sun was up, Tumpie walked two miles to the Soulard Market. The Market was a big old place, full of carrots and tomatoes and soggy wooden lettuce crates. There, she hid under the farmers' stalls and snatched up the vegetables and fruits that fell on the ground.

"I see you, Tumpie!" the farmers laughed, and Tumpie grinned.

Then, putting the apples and tomatoes into her little wagon, she'd start home, back to Gratiot Street, the poorest section of St. Louis.

This morning, as she passed the Rosebud Café on Market Street, the tinny sounds of a pianola spilled out onto the sidewalk, and inside, Tumpie could hear a red-hot mama singing "Wild Cherries."

It was the summer of 1915, and St. Louis was jumping. Music was everywhere. Ragtime music.

Tumpie dropped the wagon handle and leaned up against the café wall. Standing there in the sunlight, she listened to the strumming of the banjos, to the high-pitched cry of the clarinet, and to the tinkling of the keys as the piano man ran his fingers up the scale. The catchy rhythm jumped to her toes and her foot began tapping out the beat on the pavement.

Ragtime was piano music, happy music, and it always made Tumpie think of Eddie, her honky-tonk daddy. Eddie didn't live with them anymore. He'd moved out a long time ago, and Tumpie's stepfather had moved in. Tumpie knew her daddy wasn't coming back, but she still liked to remember all the fun they used to have, back when Eddie would whip out his sticks and set up his drums anywhere — picnics and barrel houses, riverboats and gambling halls.

At night, Tumpie's mama would take her to
the honky-tonks to hear Eddie and his friends
play. Everyone had loved watching Eddie,
especially when he'd lean back, close his eyes,
and lick the snare drum with the tips of his
sticks. Then the place would really heat up.

"Dill Pickles Rag."

"Frog Legs Rag."

"Chicken Chowder."

The catchiest music in the nation, and Tumpie
had heard it all.

In the afternoons, Eddie would stand in front
of the pool halls, strutting and showing off his
shiny new shoes. He carried his drumsticks
everywhere, and sometimes, when he wasn't
throwing dice, he'd bend down and beat the
sticks on the cracked cement.

"Hear that, honey?" he'd say to Tumpie. "That's
called syncopation!"

"Syn-co-pa-tion!" Tumpie would shout, and
she'd skip out the beat on the sidewalk.

Then Eddie would show her a two-step he'd learned at the Dance Academy, tossing his sticks high into the air, where they'd spin like fire against the sun. The two of them would start clapping and laughing, and on days like that, the whole street seemed alive with dancing and color and the fast joy of ragtime music.

Tumpie was still lost in thought when the train whistle blew. She jumped and started pulling her wagon. She knew she'd better get down to the tracks. Once a week, her stepfather, Arthur, sent her down to Union Station to pick up the coal that had fallen off the hopper cars. She didn't mind, though. The coal kept them warm at night, and besides, she liked watching the trains. The trains went everywhere.

A block away, Tumpie could hear the Knickerbocker pulling in from New York, and as she got closer to the tracks, she began thinking of all the places she'd like to see, like the dance halls in Harlem, where the girls wore fancy dresses and the jazz men played till dawn.

I wish I could get on a train and just ride away," she thought, picking up the black, dusty lumps.

As soon as the wagon was loaded up, coal on one end, fruits and vegetables on the other, Tumpie headed for home. Rounding the corner, she caught her reflection in the window of the Four Deuces Saloon. She smiled at it. Then she crossed her eyes and made a face. Someone inside started laughing, and that made her laugh, too. So, doing her daddy's two-step, she kicked out her legs and pretended she was a world-famous honky-tonker.

"I'm Ragtime Tumpie!" she laughed, and as she skipped down the sidewalk, the apples and tomatoes bounced up and down in her wagon.

By the time she got home, one of the wheels was loose and the bananas were brown from the sun. As she let herself into the apartment,

Tumpie could hear her mama and stepfather talking. Carrie's voice sounded heavy and tired, and Arthur was complaining.

"I'm home," Tumpie called, taking the bruised fruit out of the wagon and putting it on the kitchen table.

"You're late," Arthur said. "What happened?"

"Nothin'." Tumpie pushed the wagon into its corner. "Got some apricots. Real sweet, too."

Arthur grunted. "What were you doin'?" he said. "Dancing in the street again? Makin' a fool of yourself?"

Tumpie looked Arthur right in the eye, apricot juice dripping down her chin.

"I'm gonna be a honky-tonk dancer," she told him, "and I'm gonna make lots of money!"

"Oh, sure," he said. "And I'm gonna be President!"

He laughed and walked out the door.

The air that night was hot and muggy. In bed, Tumpie could hear the distant sounds of pianos and laughter, and women singing the blues in the dark: "My man done gone away. Now the blues done hit me hard . . ."

She thought of her daddy, and the barrel house banjos and the fast rags, and the hot, red lights of Chestnut Valley. Down the street, she could hear the band playing "Cotton Bolls," real slow and sad-like. She closed her eyes, and little by little, the lazy, bluesy sound of the saxophones lulled Tumpie to sleep.

The months passed. Winter came early, and the snow hung thick on the windowsills. In December, the apartment was so cold that Tumpie danced just to keep warm.

"Kick those legs up," Carrie told her, "and clap your hands. If you gonna dance, girl, you gotta have rhythm!"

Sometimes, Carrie would put down her broom and the two of them would dance together, and Tumpie would pretend they were on the stage of the Booker T. Washington Theater and that she was the star. The apartment seemed less cold then, and even Arthur stopped being such an old sourpuss.

When spring came, she kept dancing. Once a week, the neighborhood kids put on a vaudeville show, and Tumpie got to dance in the chorus. The seats were made out of orange crates and the curtain was nothing but a handful of rags, but Tumpie did the bunny hug until beads of sweat ran down her forehead and the planks of the wooden stage rattled.

"You're gonna wear out your feet, girl!" her mama told her.

But Tumpie didn't care. All summer long she danced barefoot up and down the hot St. Louis sidewalks.

Then, one morning, Medicine Man came to town. His rickety wagon was filled with colorful bottles.

"Step right up!" he said. "My potions can cure anything!"

The people in the neighborhood began to gather around.

Medicine Man stayed all day.

He sold snake oil and rheumatism tonic, and ancient powders "stolen from the Great Pyramids of Egypt."

He never stopped talking, and one by one, all of the colorful bottles were sold.

Then, darkness slowly fell. It was a hot, steamy St. Louis night. The kerosene torches were lit and someone started playing the harmonica.

Medicine Man grinned.

"We're gonna have a dancin' contest," he said.

A fiddler stepped forward. The harmonica man played faster, and everyone started clapping and stomping their feet.

Tumpie stood near the edge of the crowd and watched, her fingers drumming a fire hydrant. One by one, people climbed up onto the stage and danced to the ragtime music. Even old Savannah, heavy as she was, got up and threw her big hips around. Her bandana was a swirl of hot color.

"Can I go up?" Tumpie begged her mama.

"You're too little," Carrie whispered. "Anyway, it's time for your bed."

Just then, Medicine Man pulled something out of his hat.

"I got a shiny silver dollar for the winner," he promised.

Suddenly, Tumpie was pushing her way through the crowd.

I ain't too little!" she cried. "Oh, please, mister, oh, please, let me dance. I ain't too little!"

Medicine Man laughed and pulled her up onto the stage. The clapping and the stomping seemed to get faster and louder.

"What's your name?" he asked.

"Tumpie," she said, staring at the silver dollar.

"Well, you go to it, sweet pea," and he pushed her to the center of the stage.

The air was sharp with the smell of kerosene. At the back of the crowd, Carrie watched as the harmonica man began counting out a beat. The fiddler caught the rhythm and swung his bow, music jumped from the little harmonica, and Tumpie, barefoot and burning with excitement, started to dance.

It was a fast rag, the kind her daddy used to heat up the honky-tonks with. Real jug band jazz. Tumpie closed her eyes, kicked out her legs, and pretended she was on the stage of the Booker T. Washington Theater. The crowd roared. She clapped her hands, threw her head back, and laughed and laughed.

Then, before she knew it, before she'd hardly started, the rag was over. But the crowd was still yelling, and Tumpie was still dancing.

She felt dizzy when Medicine Man handed her the silver dollar.

"No doubt about it, you won the contest!" he grinned.

The night sky echoed with the whoops and the cheers.

"Mama," Tumpie cried, "did you hear that, Mama? He said I won! I won!" She couldn't believe it. A silver dollar! For dancing!

Carrie hugged her tight. "You were real good, Tumpie, real good."

Tumpie could hardly stand still. "I'm gonna be a dancer, Mama, that's what I'm gonna be!"

" 'Course you are, honey." Carrie took her by the hand. "Now, come on home. Why, look at you, you're all tired out."

"But, Mama—"

"Come on, Tumpie."

The crowd was breaking up. Next to the stage, someone started dousing the kerosene torches. Tumpie was still staring at the silver dollar in her hand. "I'll never stop dancin' now!"

Carrie smiled. "'Course not, sugar. Now, come on. Time for bed."

Across the street, Medicine Man had packed up his wares and was climbing into his wagon. He yawned as he took the reins in his hand.

"Giddyup," he said.

The wagon lurched forward.

As he passed by, Tumpie heard Medicine Man let out a deep sigh.

"Lord, it's been a long, long day, and heaven's still a mile away..."

Then the streets were empty and still. Blocks away, someone was singing the blues.

A cat meowed.

Tumpie slipped the silver dollar into her pocket, took Mama's hand, and the two of them set off for home.

THINKING ABOUT IT

1. Tumpie dreamed of being a dancer. What do you dream of doing? What can you do to make your dream come true?

2. "I'll never stop dancin' now!" said Tumpie. Which characters helped Tumpie with her dream? How did they help?

3. Who is the artist for this story? How did he paint pictures to give you the feeling of Tumpie dancing? How do you picture her dancing? How would you describe it to someone else?

The Early Years of Benjamin Franklin

Written Down and Illustrated by Aliki

Benjamin Franklin was born with just one life.

But as he grew, his curiosity, his sense of humor, and his brilliant mind, turned him into a man with many lives.

Benjamin Franklin was born in Boston in 1706.

His mother and his father, who was a candlemaker, had many children.

But they saw Ben was special.

He was curious.

He loved books.

And even as a child, he was full of bright ideas.

Ben was always thinking—even at play.

He liked to swim, and tried different ways.

Once he made paddles so he could go faster.

Another time, when he was flying his kite near a pond, he had another idea.

He went for a swim holding on to the kite string.

Just as he thought, the kite pulled him across the water.

Ben loved school, but his parents did not have the money for him to continue.

After only two years, he had to leave and choose a trade.

Ben's paddles were wooden, with a hole for his thumb. He made paddles for his feet, too.

Ben's job as an apprentice was to clean and sort type, sweep the floor, and sell newspapers.

Ben spent nights and Sundays reading and practicing his writing.

It was decided that Ben would learn to be a printer like his brother, James.

So when he was twelve, Ben was sent to live with him.

Ben learned quickly.

He worked long, hard hours.

Still, he found time to read every book he could borrow, and saved the money he earned to buy more.

James showed the letters to his friends.

Silence Dogood wrote that she was a poor widow with some ideas she wished to share.

She said she would write again.

I don't know who she is but I'll print them.

Clever!

Interesting!

Funny!

Another letter!

People could hardly wait for Widow Dogood's next letter.

Ben wrote more and more letters.

At the shop, Ben wanted to do more than just help print his brother's newspaper.

He wanted to write in it, too.

So he thought of a way.

James began finding mysterious letters under the office door.

They were signed "Silence Dogood."

Silence wrote such funny stories, clever essays and poetry, James printed them.

In fact, they helped him sell more newspapers.

Little did he know that Silence Dogood was his little brother Ben.

But when James found out, he was angry.

Ben was not allowed to write any more.

He decided to go somewhere else, where he could write.

So when he was 17, he left James and Boston.

Ben went to Philadelphia to start a life of his own.

He found a job with a printer.

He read and collected more books.

He worked and saved until at last he bought his own shop.

Now he could print his own newspaper and all the letters he wished.

A few years later, Ben met and married a young girl named Deborah Read.

Deborah worked hard, too.

She managed their new house, and her own general store next to Ben's print shop.

Before long they had two children to help them.

Ben's newspaper was a great success.

Then he began printing a yearly calendar called Poor Richard's Almanack.

The booklet was full of advice, news, and information.

What made it even more special were the wise, witty sayings of Poor Richard.

Year after year, people bought the almanac.

It made Ben famous.

Meanwhile, Benjamin Franklin was busy living other lives.

He loved Philadelphia.

It was a new city full of promise, and Benjamin was there at the right time.

He started a club called the Junto, where friends met to discuss books and ideas.

He lent out his books, and soon others did the same.

This began the first free lending library in America.

He found new ways to light the streets, and to have them cleaned and paved, too.

He started a police force, a fire department, a hospital, and an Academy.

He helped make laws.

Philadelphia became as famous as Benjamin Franklin.

People put "Franklin Rods" up on their rooftops in America and in other countries, too.

By the time he was forty-two, Benjamin Franklin had enough money from his printing to live in comfort with his family.

He gave up the shop to spend all his time with his ideas.

A new life began.

Ben started scientific experiments, and soon became a master.

He was the first to prove lightning was electricity.

One day, during a thunderstorm, he tried a dangerous experiment with a kite and a key, and found he was right.

He realized how to protect houses from lightning, and invented the lightning rod.

He experimented in his garden and found better ways to grow crops.

He invented glasses called bifocals. He could see far, out of the top of the glasses, and near, out of the bottom.

He introduced Swiss barley, Chinese rhubarb, Newton apples, willow for baskets, and turnips to America.

He found out that black cloth keeps one warmer than white by laying pieces of cloth in the snow. After some time, the black cloth was warmed by the sun and sank into the snow. The white didn't.

Benjamin Franklin made many discoveries in his lifetime, but he refused money for them.

He said his ideas belonged to everyone.

He wrote them down and they were translated into many languages.

He became the best-known man in America.

Thinking About It

1. Be Ben Franklin's buddy. What will you do with him? What will you say to him or ask him? Use the pictures to tell about being his buddy.

2. Benjamin Franklin invented many new things. What are some of your favorites? Which ones are still used today? Which one would you have liked to help him make?

3. Ben Franklin is coming to visit your class. What modern inventions will you show him? What will he say about them?

Meet Someone You Should Know
Young Wolfgang Amadeus Mozart amazed the world with his music in *Mozart: Scenes from the Childhood of a Great Composer* by Catherine Brighton.

HOW
DROOFUS THE
DRAGON
LOST HIS HEAD

WRITTEN AND ILLUSTRATED BY

BILL PEET

Once upon a time there lived a family of dragons. They were a horrible bunch of beasts who traveled about from country to country stirring up trouble wherever they went.

One day on a trip to some faraway land the dragon family flew into a dense fog, and Droofus, the youngest of the dragons, lost track of the others.

Droofus kept circling about in the endless gray cloud, calling and calling in a squeaky small voice until at last he was too weary to flap his wings.

Then the little dragon gave up and went gliding down to land on a mountainside and crawled into a cave where he curled up in a corner to sleep for the night.

Droofus awoke the next morning feeling very lonely and ever so hungry. So he left his cave to find something for breakfast. Droofus was just four years old, and at that age dragons feed on small things like grasshoppers and beetles. As he was searching the tall grass near the cave he came across a grasshopper struggling helplessly in a spider web.

The spider was all set to pounce when suddenly Droofus snatched the grasshopper out of the web.

For a long while Droofus held the grasshopper by one leg wondering what to do. How could he eat someone just after saving his life? It didn't seem right, so he finally set the grasshopper free.

After that Droofus gave up eating grasshoppers and beetles and all other things that hopped or crept or crawled. As much as he disliked it, the young dragon took to eating grass.

"It tastes awful," he said after one mouthful, "but I'll just have to get used to it." And sure enough, the more grass he ate the better he liked it. Pretty soon Droofus found the grass so tasty he was stuffing it down by the fistful.

And in a surprisingly short time the grass-eating dragon grew into a giant of a monster, a huge scaly brute with a long, pointed tail and big, leathery bat wings.

"There's too much of me now," grumbled Droofus. "I'm one big overgrown lunk with nothing to do but eat and sleep." Then he remembered his wings. He hadn't been on a flight since he was four years old, the day he was lost in the fog.

"Flying might be fun for a change," he said, and spreading his wings he sailed up through the pines, then on out over the countryside.

It was a perfect day for flying, so sunny and clear he could make out every haystack that dotted the fields far below.

He could see cows in the meadow, ducks in a pond, and a cart traveling along a yellow ribbon of a road past the farmhouses.

Farther on there were more roads and more houses—great clusters of houses with a castle towering above the rooftops. It was the castle of the king, and the king was out on a balcony to enjoy the beautiful morning.

"Great Gazootikens!" he cried, when he caught sight of Droofus. "A dragon! A whopper of a dragon!"

And the king watched in amazement until the dragon had sailed away to disappear in the forest high on the mountainside.

"What a marvelous thing it would be," he said, "to have that giant dragon's head on the wall of the great hall." And the king offered a reward of a hundred golden quadrooples for the dragon's head, which was a lot of money in those days.

That same afternoon every brave knight in the kingdom rode up the mountainside in search of the giant dragon.

Droofus was resting against a tree when the "clumpity clump" of horses hoofs and the "clankity clank" of armor reached his ears.

The two-ton dragon was much too weary from his sightseeing trip to go flying again, so he scurried back into his cave to hide.

The knights were looking for a cave with bones scattered about the entrance, but if they had gone all the way into one of them they would have seen Droofus.

After one peek into Droofus' cave they hurried
on up the mountainside, peeking into all the other
caves as they went. The knights searched for
months, peeking into hundreds of caves, but not
one of them had the look of a dragon's cave. So at
last they gave up in despair.

The dragon's hideout would have remained a
mystery if a lamb hadn't gone astray one evening.
The lamb had wandered into the pine forest on the
mountainside, and before long a farm boy came
looking for her. Lighting the way with a lantern,
the boy followed the lamb's trail. Small bits of wool
had caught on the brambles here and there. When
he came to a cave, he raised his lantern to peer
inside.

At first there seemed to be nothing in the cave
but rabbits. Then farther back in the dark he spied
a small white blob. It was the lamb curled up
beside a scaly, pointed dragon's tail. And looming
up to the roof of the cave was the rest of the
dragon, sound asleep and snoring.

"Here, Flossy! Come on, Flossy," the boy called softly, careful not to awaken the dragon. The lamb finally raised her head, hopped to her feet, and came trotting out of the cave. And the boy and the lamb went scampering away through the forest.

Halfway down the mountain they met the boy's father and he was very angry.

"How many times must I warn you," he growled, "to stay out of the woods after dark."

"But I had to find Flossy," said the boy, "and you'd never guess where. She was sleeping in a cave with a dragon."

"A d-d-dragon!" stammered his father. "Are-are you sure?"

"A giant of a dragon!" said the boy.

"Why, son, did you know there's a reward for his head? A hundred gold quadrooples! The king's knights have been searching the mountain for months. If you lead the knights to his cave, I'm sure you will get at least part of the reward."

"I can't do that," said the boy. "If he wouldn't hurt my lamb then he must be a good dragon. So I'll never tell anyone where he lives."

With nothing to worry about and so little to do, life was getting dull for Droofus, and he decided a change of scenery might help. One day he said good-bye to his cave and took off on a trip to most anywhere. However, he picked the very worst day for flying, and before he knew it Droofus was caught in a storm.

He wheeled around to head back for his cave— but too late. The fierce wind twisted his neck and tail and ripped at his wings and sent him tumbling backward into the clouds.

The dragon battled the storm until his wings were tattered to shreds. Then, helpless as a butterfly, he went whirling down out of the clouds to land with an earth-shaking "Ker-whump" far out in a field.

Droofus was so badly battered and bruised he couldn't move. He was one big hurt from the point on his tail to the spikes on his nose. And he lay there sprawled out in the field while the storm went thundering away over the mountains.

Then he heard someone shouting, "It's the dragon! The big dragon! I saw him fall!" And pretty soon a small boy came running across the field, followed by a man and a woman. It was the same boy who had found his lamb in the dragon's cave.

"It's him all right," said the boy, after one look at Droofus.

"He appears to be dead," said his father.

"What a pitiful big thing," said his mother.

"But he's not dead," cried the boy. "He just blinked an eye!"

"I can blink an eye," groaned Droofus, "but that's all. I'm just about done for."

"Are you going to tell the king," the boy asked his father, "and collect the hundred quadrooples?"

"You found him, son. So that's for you to decide."

"He's a good dragon," said the boy, "and if I take good care of him he might get well."

Droofus was covered with a strawstack to keep him from chilling during the night. And every day the boy brought him bunches of fresh grass and a tub of fresh water. And every day the dragon felt a bit better.

"What makes your father so sad?" asked Droofus one day.

"Because we're so poor," said the boy. "And the reason we are poor is because of all these big rocks. They take up so much room there's not much land left to grow anything. We've tried every which way to get rid of them. But with everyone on the farm all pulling and pushing at once we can't budge even one of the rocks."

"That is enough to make anyone sad," sighed Droofus.

Early one morning, long before the first rooster crow, Droofus burst out of the strawstack feeling as fit as ever and just as good as new, except for his wings.

They were still so badly tattered they were useless. But the wings didn't matter. After that awful crash landing Droofus was through with flying. Besides, he had better things to do.

Seizing the nearest boulder in his powerful claws he jerked it off the ground, then carried it away to the far end of the field where he dropped it "Ker-blump!"

"That was easy," said Droofus. The next time he carried three rocks, then four and five, stacking them all into one pile. When the poor farmer stepped out of the door of his cottage that morning the land was half cleared, and he let out a "Whoop!" that could be heard for a mile.

"I told you he was a good dragon," said the boy.

"He's a great dragon!" cried his father, tossing his hat high in the air.

By noontime Droofus had piled every last rock into one big pyramid. At last the land was clear, and the happy farmer hitched his donkey to a plow and set out across the field.

"If that's what you call plowing," said the dragon, "I can do that too."

Jabbing his pointed tail deep into the ground, Droofus went trotting along, leaving a deep furrow, pulling up the weeds and eating them as he went.

After the plowing was done he helped plant the wheat. He hauled logs from the forest, and using his long jagged tail for a saw, he cut enough firewood in one day to last the whole winter. When he ran out of things to do he stood in the wheatfield with his great arms outstretched serving as a very fine scarecrow.

"He's worth a lot more than a hundred quadrooples," said the happy farmer. "He's worth a thousand."

But the happiest of all was Droofus. At last he had become something useful, not just a big lunk of a thing. He no longer worried about the king's knights coming after him. The farm was so far out in the country hardly anyone knew it was there.

The only one to worry about was an old sheepherder who lived somewhere back in the hills. Once every spring the man drove his oxcart over the bumpy road that ran past the farm on his way to the village to market his wool.

The bad-tempered old fellow could be heard
shouting at his oxen long before he passed by the
farm. So there was plenty of time for Droofus to
slip out of sight behind the barn.

But one spring day as the oxcart passed by,
Droofus was careless and left his long, pointed tail
sticking out. The old sheepherder knew very well
that such a tail could only belong to a dragon.
When he reached the village late in the day, the old
fellow went straight to the castle to tell the king.

The next day the king and all his knights came
riding up the road to the farm on their great war
horses, armed with swords and lances.

Droofus knew there was no use hiding. They had heard he was there or they wouldn't have come. So he stood there in the field while the farmer and his son ran out to meet them.

"We've come for the dragon," said the king, "and here's your reward of a hundred golden quadrooples."

"I don't want the reward," said the farmer. "The dragon's not for sale."

"I must have his head," said the king, "so please stand aside."

"But he's a good dragon," said the boy. "He's as tame as a kitten. He even sleeps by my bed every night."

"Look here, boy," growled the king, "I've got no time for tomfoolery."

"Oh, I didn't mean all of him," said the boy. "Only his head sleeps by my bed. He sticks his neck through the window and the rest of him stays outside."

"Well now, son, that's a bit more like it," said the king. "In fact, that gives me an idea. A grand idea! I'll borrow your dragon just for special occasions, and I'll pay you twenty quadrooples each time. What do you say to that?"

"It's up to the dragon," said the boy.

"Make it thirty quadrooples," said Droofus.

"Then thirty it is," said the king.

Droofus made his first visit to the king's castle on the eighth day of April, the day of the Grand Spring Festival. People came from miles around, crowding into the great hall, which was splendorously bedecked with banners and streamers and festoons of flowers. High up on the wall a giant of a dragon's head appeared through an elegant window framed in gold. A happy, smiling dragon's head that brought cries of surprise and squeals of delight and sent the crowd into a jolly frolicsome mood. Soon they were all singing and dancing to the music of trumpets and flutes and the Spring Festival was going full tilt.

The dragon was so carried away by all the merriment he suddenly burst into song with a booming, earsplitting voice that rocked the rafters and drowned out all the trumpets and flutes before he finally caught himself. In all the excitement Droofus the Dragon lost his head—but only for a moment.

THINKING ABOUT IT

1.

What would happen if Droofus flew into your neighborhood? What would you and your neighbors do?

2.

The boy who found Droofus in the cave kept it a secret. Why did he do that? Do you agree with him? Why?

3.

Bill Peet shows Droofus feeling different ways. Which picture is your favorite? How is Droofus feeling in the picture? How could another picture show a different feeling?

NO SUCH THINGS

WRITTEN
AND
ILLUSTRATED

by BILL PEET

The common big wig-tailed Mopwoggins
Have no hair at all on their noggins.
That's the main reason why they're so sheepish
    and shy.
And also the reason they are crafty
    and sly.

They hide their bare heads in a very strange way,

By using their tails as a perfect toupee.

And no one would guess that their noggins were
  hairless,

If the sheepish Mopwoggins were not sometimes
  careless.

It's no fun for the Flumpers to crawl on the ground,
So they coil themselves up to be perfectly round.
Then they go for a spin, a wild, whirling ride,
Far out in the hilly, broad countryside.

After so many miles of rolling about,

They discover their rubbery hides have worn out.

Since they can't be retreaded once they go flat,

There's nothing the Flumpers can do after that.

The golden-brown crested, pie-faced Pazeeks
Have huge appetites to match their big beaks.
And their three-toed, unusual, pitchfork-like feet
Are perfect for picking the cherries they eat.

To make sure everyone in the flock gets his share,
There's a strict pecking order to keep it all fair.
This means that the smaller ones stay in their
    places
Till the bigger Pazeeks are done filling their
    faces.

The spooky-tailed Tizzy has a brain that's so
    small,
She forgets everything in just no time
    at all.
That is why her own tail is a shocking surprise,
With its ferocious jaws and enormous red eyes.

70

One glimpse of the thing and she lets out a shriek,

Flies into a Tizzy, takes off like a streak.

She runs on for miles just screaming in terror,

Before she discovers her horrible error.

The Skeezaboos' skis are completely self-grown,

So you might say these skiers ski on their own.

Ker-swoosh! They take off in a smooth,
easy glide,

Aboard their big horns down a steep
mountainside.

The Skeezaboos could have a wonderful time

If the return trip weren't such a torturous climb.

When the horns hook on snags and keep bumping
  their knees,

Then they wish they weren't quite so attached to
  their skis.

If the fancy Fandangos seem stuck-up and snooty,
It is mostly because of their exquisite beauty.
They're most often seen with smug, smiling faces,
By a crystal-clear pond in a jungle oasis.

There they linger for hours with nothing to do
But sip the sweet water and admire the view.
And the view they admire, as you might well
suppose,
Is their own reflection, right under
their nose.

Bill Peet, age 11

DRAWING: A HABIT-FORMING HOBBY

BY BILL PEET

Bill Peet

Bill Peet, the author and illustrator of How Droofus the Dragon Lost His Head *and* No Such Things, *grew up in Indianapolis, Indiana. He lived with his mother, grandmother, and two brothers in a house on North Riley Avenue. In this excerpt from his autobiography, Bill Peet talks about the time he spent drawing when he was a boy.*

That house on North Riley Avenue was where I spent the happiest years of my boyhood.

My favorite room in the house was an attic, where I enjoyed filling fat five-cent tablets with a hodgepodge of drawings. Drawing became my number one hobby as soon as I could manipulate a crayon or pencil well enough to put my favorite things on paper.

I have no idea how well I drew then since all those early drawings are long gone. However, I must have drawn fairly well or I couldn't have enjoyed it so much.

I drew for hours at a time just for the fun of it, and yet I was hoping to find some practical reason to draw for the rest of my life. But when I entered grade school, my drawing habit suddenly became a problem.

There was an art class once a week but that wasn't nearly enough, and no fun at all. The art teacher decided what we were to draw, and they were never my kind of things.

So I drew on the sly in all my other classes by hiding a tablet in my desk and sneaking a drawing into it now and then. Very often I'd get caught at it, and the teacher would snatch my tablet away and warn me to stick to my studies.

I also drew in the margins of the pages, which was graphic evidence that I had spent very little time reading the text.

But when it came time for the used book sales, my illustrated books were best sellers. The kids loved my drawings, and I suppose those books could be considered the very first ones I ever illustrated for children.

THINKING ABOUT IT

1. Bill Peet created many strange and funny creatures in *No Such Things*. Which one would you like to be for a day? Why? What would you do as one of the creatures?

2. Have a chat with Bill Peet. What will you ask him? Why?

3. You are creating a new No Such Thing. What will you call it? Describe how it looks and what it does.

MORE FROM BILL PEET'S IMAGINATION
Cyrus sets out to prove he is more than a spineless sea serpent in *Cyrus the Unsinkable Sea Serpent*.

TOO MUCH NOISE

a folk tale retold as a play by Marilyn Price

CHARACTERS: NARRATOR

      WOMAN

      WISE ONE

      DOG

      COW

      TWO RELATIVES

      FRIEND

      CURIOUS NEIGHBOR

NARRATOR: Once upon a time there lived a woman in a little house all by herself. Now the Woman was never lonely. She enjoyed her own company, and her little house was just right for her. She did, however, have one little problem.

WOMAN: MY HOUSE IS TOO NOISY! At night when I climb into my bed, I put my head on the pillow and close my eyes, but I can't fall asleep. The minute I put my head on the pillow, the leaves on the roof go RUSTLE, RUSTLE, RUSTLE! and the bed goes SQUEAK! and the floor goes CREAK! and I can't sleep—MY HOUSE IS TOO NOISY!

NARRATOR: After trying a variety of methods to fall asleep and finding none that worked, the Woman decided to leave the house in the middle of the night and visit the Wise One in the town to ask for some advice. And so she did. She walked to the house of the Wise One and knocked on the door.

WISE ONE: Good day, I mean good night. What brings you to my house in the middle of the night, old friend?

WOMAN: I have a problem, Wise One.

WISE ONE: You have come to the right place. I will certainly do my best and wisest to help you.

WOMAN: I can't sleep. My house is too noisy.

WISE ONE: Explain this to me, please.

WOMAN: Well, every night when I put my head on my pillow, the leaves on the roof go RUSTLE, RUSTLE, RUSTLE! and the bed goes SQUEAK! and the floor goes CREAK! and I simply cannot fall asleep because MY HOUSE IS TOO NOISY!

WISE ONE: I see, or rather, I hear your problem, old friend. What you need to do is to find out what your dog does while all this is happening.

WOMAN:	My dog?
WISE ONE:	Yes, your dog. What does your dog do when you can't sleep?
WOMAN:	I don't have a dog.
WISE ONE:	No dog? Well then you had better get one.
WOMAN:	What a wonderful idea, Wise One! I would never have thought of that myself. I'll get a dog.
NARRATOR:	The Woman walked all over town in the middle of the night looking for a dog. She finally found one. She took the dog into her little house and gave him a place of his own to rest. Then the Woman put her own head on the pillow, and the leaves on the roof went RUSTLE, RUSTLE, RUSTLE! and the bed went SQUEAK! and the floor went CREAK! and the Dog went
DOG:	WOOF!

WOMAN: I don't think this is working. It seems to be even noisier than before. I had better visit the Wise One again. Come on, Dog.

DOG: WOOF!

NARRATOR: And so they went. The Woman and the Dog walked over to the other side of town and knocked on the door of the Wise One. He came downstairs, rubbing his eyes.

WISE ONE: Hello, old friend. How's your problem coming along?

WOMAN: I think it might be worse.

WISE ONE: How so? Didn't you get a dog?

WOMAN: Yes, I did exactly as you suggested. Here's my Dog. I took him into my house, and when I put my head on my pillow, the leaves on the roof went RUSTLE, RUSTLE, RUSTLE! and the bed went SQUEAK! and the floor went CREAK! and now the Dog says

DOG: WOOF! WOOF!

WOMAN: You see, Wise One, my house is noisier than before.

WISE ONE: This is very interesting, my friend, and I can certainly understand your problem. But I think that this time I have an easy solution.

WOMAN: Thank goodness!

WISE ONE: I think that, although the Dog is a fine pet to live with, you really need some animal that leads a more regularly scheduled life—like a cow!

WOMAN: A cow?

WISE ONE: Yes, a cow. You know a cow regularly gives milk and understands the time of day. Get yourself a nice cow and bring it into your house. Unless you already have a cow in the house.

WOMAN: No, I don't have a cow, and if I did, I would never have thought to bring it into my house. Where will I find a cow in the middle of the night? Cows sleep at night!

WISE ONE: Of course they do. That's why you should get a cow.

NARRATOR: After giving the Woman that bit of wisdom, the Wise One went back to bed. The Woman and the Dog went off to find a cow to bring into the house. They found one sleeping in a pasture and brought her home.

WOMAN: Well, here we are—one Dog, one Cow and one very tired Woman—in a house that seems a lot smaller than it used to. But I can't worry about that now. I have to get some sleep. Are we all comfortable?

Cow:	MOO!
Dog:	WOOF!
Narrator:	The Woman put her head on the pillow, and the leaves on the roof went RUSTLE, RUSTLE, RUSTLE! and the bed went SQUEAK! and the floor went CREAK! and the Dog said
Dog:	WOOF! WOOF!
Narrator:	and now the Cow said
Cow:	MOO!
Woman:	Far be it from me to doubt the wisdom of the Wise One, but this does not seem to be working out! Let's go, Dog and Cow. We are walking over to the other side of town to find out why the solution to this problem is not working.
Narrator:	And so they did.

WISE ONE: Hello, hello, and hello. What a sight in the middle of the night. How are you all?

WOMAN: Well, Wise One, to tell you the truth, and I always do, I am a little tired. Actually, I am a lot tired. I did exactly as you said. I got a Dog. I got a reliable Cow. I brought them both into my house. This is what happened when I put my head on my pillow: the leaves on the roof went RUSTLE, RUSTLE, RUSTLE! and the bed went SQUEAK! and the floor went CREAK! and the Dog said

DOG: WOOF! WOOF!

WOMAN: and now the Cow says

COW: MOO!

WOMAN: My house, with all respect Wise One, is noisier than ever!

WISE ONE: My mistake. You are absolutely right. What can you tell from the Cow or the Dog as nice as they are? You were very patient with me. What I recommend to you now is a little human company.

WOMAN: Human company? What do you mean?

WISE ONE: Do you have any friends or relatives that need a place to sleep or someone to talk with?

WOMAN: There is always someone I could find to take home with me, but then what?

WISE ONE: Why, settle them into your house and then try to get some sleep. You look exhausted!

NARRATOR: On the way back to her little house, the Woman found two Relatives, one Friend, and a Curious Neighbor. She invited them all to spend the night in her little house. They accepted with gratitude. Now the strange parade of one Woman, one Dog, one Cow, two Relatives, one Friend, and one Curious Neighbor marched across town in the middle of the night. They barely fit into the Woman's house.

WOMAN: Here we are. Make yourselves at home. I am going to try to get some sleep.

NARRATOR: The Woman put her head on the pillow, and the leaves on the roof went RUSTLE, RUSTLE, RUSTLE! and the bed went SQUEAK! and the floor went CREAK! and the Dog said

DOG: WOOF! WOOF!

NARRATOR: and the Cow said

COW: MOO!

NARRATOR: and the two Relatives, one Friend, and one Curious Neighbor sat up and said together

ALL: THIS HOUSE IS TOO NOISY!

NARRATOR: And with the Woman, the Dog, and the Cow, they marched out of the house and over to the house of the Wise One. Together they banged on his door.

WISE ONE: Look at this group—what a crowd! Such a party! But old friend, you look terrible, more tired than ever. Did you do everything exactly as I had recommended?

WOMAN: I paid very careful attention, and I did exactly as you said. First I got a Dog.

DOG: WOOF!

WOMAN: Then I got a Cow.

COW: MOO!

WOMAN: Then I found two Relatives, one Friend, and one Curious Neighbor, and I invited them all in.

ALL: HER HOUSE IS TOO NOISY!

WOMAN:	And now it's worse than ever! The leaves on the roof go RUSTLE, RUSTLE, RUSTLE! and the bed goes SQUEAK! and the floor goes CREAK! and the Dog says
DOG:	WOOF!
WOMAN:	and the Cow says
COW:	MOO!
WOMAN:	And now these people say
ALL:	HER HOUSE IS TOO NOISY!
WOMAN:	Please, Wise One, what should I do? I am very tired.
WISE ONE:	The solution is simple.
WOMAN:	It is?

WISE ONE: Absolutely. Your friends think it is too noisy, right?

WOMAN: Right.

WISE ONE: Then send them home.

WOMAN: Good idea.

WISE ONE: The Cow stays up and moos, right?

WOMAN: She certainly does.

WISE ONE: She needs to sleep. Send her back to her pasture!

WOMAN: It's getting better.

WISE ONE: The Dog seems to be keeping you up with his barking, right?

WOMAN: He barks all the time!

WISE ONE: He probably wants to be out roaming. Let him roam!

WOMAN: Then what?

WISE ONE: Then listen to how your house sounds.

NARRATOR: The Woman did exactly as the Wise One told her. She said to her human companions

WOMAN: Good night. Come again, but PLEASE come in the daytime.

ALL: Good night!

NARRATOR: She put the Cow out to pasture.

COW: MOO!

NARRATOR: She let the Dog out to roam the countryside. Then she went to bed. She put her head on the pillow and even though the leaves on the roof still went RUSTLE, RUSTLE, RUSTLE! and the bed still went SQUEAK! and the floor still went CREAK! she fell sound asleep, because it didn't seem so noisy after all!

THINKING ABOUT IT

1. QUIET DOWN!! What makes a lot of noise at your home? What do you do when it gets too noisy?

2. Dogs and cows don't seem quiet. How did adding noisy animals and people at home help the woman? Was this the best solution? Why?

3. It's quiet now but the woman can't sleep. Now she thinks there's too much light. What advice will the Wise One give her?

ANOTHER CREATIVE SOLUTION
Otis Crampton finds a clever use for all the junk in the town dump in *Stay Away from the Junkyard* by Tricia Tusa.

PUPPET PLAY

by Marilyn Price

The play *Too Much Noise* comes from a very old Eastern European folk tale called "It Could Be Worse." When I decided to change it into a play, I thought it would be fun to use puppets to present the play. The steps below tell how I make tube puppets. You can make them too. Just follow these directions.

Collect the following things you will need:

Construction paper   Tape   Yarn and cloth
Markers or crayons   Scissors   Imagination

1 To make the body of the puppet, roll a piece of construction paper loosely around your arm. Make sure your arm will fit inside the tube, because that is how you will hold and move the puppet. (You may want a friend to help you with this part.)

2 Tape the tube together using one long piece of tape.

3 To make the puppet's head, cut a strip of construction paper long enough to wrap around the tube and draw a face in the middle of the strip. Keep the face simple.

4 Wrap the face around the tube. Tape it in place.

5 Decorate the puppet with yarn, markers, and cloth. Add strips of paper for arms if you want.

When I want to make an animal puppet, I just turn the tube sideways, add four legs, and, using lots of imagination, decorate it.

Making these tube puppets is fun, but I also enjoy deciding how each puppet's voice will sound when the play is performed. How will the Wise One sound? the Woman? Try using your imagination to come up with interesting voices for these characters. Have fun performing *Too Much Noise* with your puppets!

The Engineer

by A. A. Milne

Let it rain!
Who cares?
I've a train
Upstairs,
With a brake
Which I make
From a string
Sort of thing,
Which works
In jerks,
'Cos it drops
In the spring,
Which stops
With the string,

And the wheels
All stick
So quick
That it feels
Like a thing
That you make
With a brake,
Not string. . . .

So that's what I make,
When the day's all wet.
It's a good sort of brake
But it hasn't worked yet.

A Bicycle for Rosaura

Written by Daniel Barbot
Illustrations by Morella Fuenmayor

Señora Amelia loved animals. At home she had a dog, a kitten, a talking parrot, a turtle, twin canaries and a handsome hen named Rosaura.

The month before Rosaura's birthday, Señora Amelia asked, "Have you decided what you'd like for your birthday?"

"Why, yes. A bicycle!" said Rosaura.

"But that's impossible!" Señora Amelia exclaimed. "Who's ever heard of a hen riding a bicycle?"

"That's just it," Rosaura replied. "I want
to be the first!"

Señora Amelia wanted to please her hen.
"Tomorrow I will try to find a bicycle for
Rosaura," she decided.

Early the next morning she took the bus into the city and stopped in all the bicycle shops. In each and every one she got the same response.

"What? A bicycle for a hen?"

Or, "No way. We don't carry any such model."

Or, "Let's take a look in the catalog. Sorry, señora. They don't make bikes for hens."

So Señora Amelia went home sad and disappointed.

"Rosaura is going to be awfully upset if I have to tell her that I couldn't find her a bicycle," she thought.

As the days passed, Señora Amelia began to think that it *was* hopeless.

Then, one afternoon a strange-looking man came into town. He walked up and down the streets singing and calling:

"I mend old clocks and jack-in-the-boxes.

I repair harmonicas and wind-chimes.

I sharpen penknives and sewing scissors.

I make rollerskates for dogs and eyeglasses for cats."

"Maybe that man can help me," thought Señora Amelia.

And she called him over right away.

"What can I do for you señora?" asked
the man. "Would you like a singing spoon,
a lunar calendar, a chocolate rocking
chair . . . . ?"

"No, no," interrupted Señora Amelia.
"What I need is . . . a bicycle for my hen."

"Umm . . . Hmmm," murmured the man.
"That is a difficult order. I'll have to take
measurements. I need to know the length
of her legs and the span of her wings."

After jotting down numbers and working
out complicated formulas, the man was
pleased to announce that he could have the
bicycle finished in time for Rosaura's
birthday.

The days seemed endless.

Finally, one morning there was a knock at her door. Señora Amelia peeked outside . . . and saw the wonderful bicycle for Rosaura!

She wrapped it up in a big box, tied a bright red ribbon around it, and on the day of Rosaura's birthday . . .

Well, Rosaura was delighted with her
present.

Now, every morning she rides to the grocery store to buy milk and bread for Señora Amelia.

So, if you should ever visit this town in Venezuela, you're sure to see Rosaura speeding by on her bicycle. But . . . watch out! The strange man forgot the brakes!

PULLING IT ALL TOGETHER

1. Rollerskates for dogs? Singing spoons? Chocolate rocking chairs?! What would you ask the strange man to make for you? Why?

2. In this book, people use their imaginations to solve some problems. What problems do you need to solve? Which characters would you go to for help? Why?

3. You're starting a museum for imagination. You may put one thing from each story in your museum. What will you choose? What will you include in your museum to show your own imagination?

BOOKS TO ENJOY

**Really Rosie
starring the Nutshell Kids**
*Written and illustrated by
Maurice Sendak
Music by Carole King*

Rosie's a star, and she's going to
make a movie of her life! Her movie
won't be complete until the rest of
the kids in the neighborhood join in.

Emma
*by Wendy Kesselman
Illustrations by Barbara Cooney*

It was Emma's birthday. She was
seventy-two years old. It was also the
day she began to paint, have new
friends, and begin a whole new life.

118

Gerald-Not-Practical
Written and illustrated by
Helena Clare Pittman

Gerald's parents want him to do something practical. Gerald wants to paint pictures. Gerald shows them that doing what you love may be the most practical thing of all.

Raggin': A Story about Scott Joplin
by Barbara Mitchell

Talk about ragtime music, and Scott Joplin's name is sure to come up. This is the story of the ragtime composer whose music still sets toes tapping.

The Boy of the Three-Year Nap
by Dianne Snyder
Illustrations by Allen Say

Taro is the laziest person in his Japanese village. His mother wants him to get a job, but he dreams of getting rich without lifting a finger. "Cheer up," he says, "I have a plan."

LITERARY TERMS

Biography

"The Early Years of Benjamin Franklin" is the story of the first half of Benjamin Franklin's life. The story of a real person's life is called a **biography.** *Ragtime Tumpie* is a biography that tells about Josephine Baker's childhood.

Humor

Some stories are funny because they don't make sense. *A Bicycle for Rosaura* is that kind of story. Can you imagine a hen riding a bicycle? The idea of a dog on roller skates or a cat wearing glasses is just as funny. Authors sometimes use impossible happenings to give **humor** to a story.

Mood

When you read a story like *Ragtime Tumpie*, it gives you a very special feeling. That is the **mood** of the story. The pictures show smiling people singing and dancing. The pictures and the words give the story a happy mood.

Onomatopoeia

Some words mean just what they sound like. In *Too Much Noise*, the leaves *rustle*, the bed goes *squeak*, and the floor goes *creak*. Say those words with a voice that makes them sound like what they mean. Can you hear the rustle of leaves? Words like *rustle*, *creak*, and *squeak* are called **onomatopoeia** (on′ə mat′ə pē′ə). What are some other words that are examples of onomatopoeia?

GLOSSARY

Words from your stories

ap·pe·tite (ap′ə tīt), **1** a desire for food: *Swimming seems to increase my appetite.* **2** a desire: *The lively children had a great appetite for adventure. noun.*

bat·ter (bat′ər), to strike with repeated blows so as to bruise, break, or get out of shape; pound: *The fireman battered down the door with an ax. verb.*

beast (bēst), **1** any four-footed animal. Lions, bears, cows, and horses are beasts. A **beast of burden** is an animal used for carrying loads: *The prairie was full of buffalo and other beasts.* **2** a cruel or brutal person. *noun.*

beast (def. 1)
Bison were **beasts** of the prairie.

blues (blüz), **1** a slow, sad song with jazz rhythm: *Bessie Smith was a famous blues singer.* **2 the blues,** low spirits: *A rainy day always gives me the blues. noun plural.*

boul·der (bōl′dər), a large rock, rounded or worn by the action of water and weather: *The ice age left many huge boulders in New England fields. noun.*

brake (brāk), **1** anything used to slow or stop the motion of a wheel or vehicle by pressing or scraping, or by rubbing against: *We heard the screech of brakes outside and ran to the window.* **2** to slow or stop by using a brake: *The driver braked the speeding car and it slid to a stop.* **1** *noun,* **2** *verb,* **brakes, braked, brak·ing.**

bruise (brüz), **1** an injury to the body, caused by a fall or a blow, that does not break the skin: *The bruise turned black-and-blue.* **2** an injury to the outside of a fruit, vegetable, or plant. **3** to injure or be injured on the outside: *Rough handling bruised the apples. My legs bruise easily.* **1,2** *noun,* **3** *verb,* **bruis·es, bruised, bruis·ing.**

ca·fe or **ca·fé** (ka fā′), a place to buy and eat a meal; restaurant: *Shall we meet at the café for dinner? noun.*

a hat	o hot	ch child	ə stands for:
ā age	ō open	ng long	a in about
ä far	ô order	sh she	e in taken
e let	oi oil	th thin	i in pencil
ē equal	ou out	ᴛʜ then	o in lemon
ėr term	u cup	zh measure	u in circus
i it	u̇ put		
ī ice	ü rule		

coil (koil), **1** to wind around and around into a pile, a tube, or a curl: *The snake coiled itself around the branch. The wire spring was evenly coiled.* **2** anything that is coiled. One wind or turn of a coil is a single coil. **1** *verb,* **2** *noun.*

coil (def. 2)
a **coil** of rope

cur·i·ous (kyu̇r′ē əs), eager to know: *Small children are very curious, and they ask many questions.* adjective.

er·ror (er′ər), **1** a mistake; something done that is wrong; something that is not the way it ought to be: *I failed my test because of errors in spelling.* **2** in baseball, a fielder's mistake that either allows a batter to reach first, or a runner to advance one or more bases. *noun.*

es·say (es′ā), a short composition on a particular subject: *Sheila wrote an essay on sleeping late.* noun.

fe·ro·cious (fə rō′shəs), fierce; savage; very cruel: *I was frightened when I saw the ferocious-looking statue.* adjective.

flock (flok), **1** a group of animals of one kind keeping, feeding, or herded together: *A flock of birds landed in our backyard.* **2** a large number; crowd: *Visitors came in flocks to the zoo to see the new gorilla.* **3** to go in a group; crowd: *The sheep flocked together. The children flocked around the ice-cream stand.* **1,2** noun, **3** verb.

hide·out (hīd′out′), a place for hiding: *The spy had a hideout on the border.* noun.

hu·man (hyü′mən), **1** of persons; that people have: *Kindness is a human trait. To know what will happen in the future is beyond human power.* **2** a person; human being: *Humans have large brains.* **1** adjective, **2** noun.

jot (jot), to write briefly or in haste: *The waiter jotted down our order.* *verb,* **jots, jot·ted, jot·ting.**

meas·ure·ment (mezh′ər mənt), **1** a measuring; finding the size, quantity, or amount: *The measurement of length by a yardstick is easy.* **2** a size, quantity, or amount found by measuring: *The measurements of the room are 10-by-15 feet.* **3** a system of measuring or of measures: *Metric measurement is used in most countries. noun.*

nois·y (noi′zē), **1** making much noise: *a noisy crowd, a noisy machine.* **2** full of noise: *It was too noisy in the den to study, so I went upstairs. adjective,* **nois·i·er, nois·i·est.**

oc·ca·sion (ə kā′zhən), **1** a particular time: *We have met them on several occasions.* **2** a special event: *The crown jewels were worn only on special occasions, such as a royal wedding.* **3** a good chance; opportunity: *The trip we took together gave us an occasion to get better acquainted. noun.*

pas·ture (pas′chər), **1** a grassy field or hillside; grassy land on which cattle, sheep, or horses can feed: *Pat turned the horses out into the pasture.* **2** grass and other growing plants: *These lands supply good pasture.* **3** to put cattle, sheep, or horses out to pasture: *The farmer pastured his cattle near the stream.* **1,2** *noun,* **3** *verb,* **pas·tures, pas·tured, pas·tur·ing.**

pave·ment (pāv′mənt), **1** a covering or surface for streets, sidewalks, or driveways, made of asphalt, concrete, gravel, or stones: *The artists set out their work on the pavement.* **2** a paved road. *noun.*

pavement (def. 1)

a hat	o hot	ch child	ə stands for:
ā age	ō open	ng long	a in about
ä far	ô order	sh she	e in taken
e let	oi oil	th thin	i in pencil
ē equal	ou out	ŦH then	o in lemon
ėr term	u cup	zh measure	u in circus
i it	ù put		
ī ice	ü rule		

pi·a·no·la (pē′ə nō′lə), a piano that plays by itself, or mechanically; a player piano: *Reggie sat down at the pianola while we got ready to dance.* noun.

pianola

please (plēz), **1** to be agreeable or be agreeable to; give pleasure: *Toys please children. Such a fine meal cannot fail to please.* **2** to wish; think fit: *Do what you please.* **3** to be so kind as to; be good or nice enough to. *Please* is used with requests and commands as a means of being polite. *Would you please go to the store for some milk? Please come here.* verb, **pleas·es, pleased, pleas·ing.**

po·tion (pō′shən), a drink, especially one used as a medicine or poison, or in magic: *"Drink this magic potion,"* whispered the magician. noun.

pounce (pouns), **1** to jump suddenly and seize: *The cat pounced upon the mouse.* **2** a sudden swoop. **1** *verb,* **pounc·es, pounced, pounc·ing; 2** *noun.*

print·er (prin′tər), **1** a person whose business or work is printing or setting type: *The books will be produced at the printer.* **2** a machine that prints, controlled by a computer. noun.

prob·lem (prob′ləm), **1** a question; difficult question: *How to do away with poverty is a problem that concerns the government.* **2** a matter of doubt or difficulty: *The president of a large company has to deal with many problems.* **3** something to be worked out: *a problem in arithmetic.* **1-3** *noun.*

rag·time (rag′tīm′), a form of jazz music, especially for piano: *Scott Joplin was a ragtime composer.* noun.

rec·om·mend (rek′ə mend′), **1** to speak in favor of; suggest favorably: *The teacher recommended her for the job. Can you recommend a good adventure story?* **2** to advise: *The doctor recommended that the patient stay in bed. verb.*

re·pair (ri per′ or ri par′), **1** to put in good condition again; mend: *He repairs shoes.* **2** an act of repairing or the work of repairing: *Repairs on the school building are made during the summer.* **3** a condition; state; shape: *The house was in very bad repair.* **1** *verb,* **2,3** *noun.*

re·sponse (ri spons′), **1** an answer by word or act: *Her response to my letter was prompt. She laughed in response to his joke.* **2** a reaction by a living thing to some change in its surroundings: *When you step into a bright light, the pupils of your eyes grow smaller in response. noun.*

re·tread (rē tred′), to put a new tread on a worn tire: *Three of our car's tires need retreading. verb,* **re·tread·ed, re·tread·ing.**

rhythm (riŦH′əm), any movement with a regular repetition of a beat, accent, rise and fall, or the like: *The band's music had a terrific rhythm. noun.*

so·lu·tion (sə lü′shən), **1** the solving of a problem: *That problem was hard; its solution required many hours.* **2** an explanation: *The police are seeking a solution of the crime.* **3** a liquid or mixture formed by dissolving: *Every time you put sugar in lemonade you are making a solution. noun.*

span (span), **1** the distance between two supports: *The bridge had a fifty-foot span.* **2** a space of time, often short or limited: *the span of human life.* **3** to extend over: *A bridge spanned the river.* **4** the distance between the tip of a person's thumb and the tip of the little finger when the hand is spread out. **1,2,4** *noun,* **3** *verb,* **spans, spanned, span·ning.**

span (def. 3)
Suspension bridges **span**
bodies of water.

a hat	o hot	ch child	ə stands for:
ā age	ō open	ng long	a in about
ä far	ô order	sh she	e in taken
e let	oi oil	th thin	i in pencil
ē equal	ou out	ŦH then	o in lemon
ėr term	u cup	zh measure	u in circus
i it	ů put		
ī ice	ü rule		

syn·co·pa·tion (sing′kə pā′shən), a musical rhythm in which the beats that are usually unaccented are given emphasis: *The dancers moved to the lively syncopation of the jazz orchestra.* noun.

tat·tered (tat′ərd), **1** torn; ragged: *The flag hung in tattered pieces after the violent wind storm.* **2** wearing torn or ragged clothes. *adjective.*

trade (trād), **1** a buying and selling; exchange of goods; commerce: *The United States has much trade with foreign countries.* **2** to exchange; make an exchange: *He traded a stick of gum for a ride on her bicycle. If you don't like your book, I'll trade with you.* **3** a kind of work; business, especially one requiring skilled work: *Josie is going into the carpenter's trade.* **1,3** *noun,* **2** *verb,* **trades, trad·ed, trad·ing.**

trade in, to give an automobile, refrigerator, or other article as payment or part payment for something, especially for a newer model.

vaude·ville (vôd′vil), an old-time form of entertainment, consisting of a variety of acts, including singing, dancing, comedy, etc.: *The school put on a vaudeville show for the spring fair.* noun.

vaudeville

ACKNOWLEDGMENTS

Text

Pages 6–28: From *Ragtime Tumpie* by Alan Schroeder with paintings by Bernie Fuchs. Text copyright © 1989 by Alan Schroeder. Illustrations copyright © 1989 by Bernie Fuchs. Reprinted by permission of Little, Brown and Company.

Pages 30–40: From *The Many Lives of Benjamin Franklin* by Aliki. Copyright © 1977, 1988 by Aliki. Used by permission of the publisher, Simon and Schuster Books for Young Readers, New York.

Pages 42–62: From *How Droofus the Dragon Lost His Head* by Bill Peet. Copyright © 1976 by William B. Peet. Reprinted by permission of Houghton Mifflin Company.

Pages 64–74: From *No Such Things* by Bill Peet. Copyright © 1983 by Bill Peet. Reprinted by permission of Houghton Mifflin Company.

Pages 76–78: From *Bill Peet: An Autobiography* by Bill Peet. Copyright © 1989 by William Peet. Reprinted by permission of Houghton Mifflin Company.

Pages 80–98: *Too Much Noise* by Marilyn Price. Copyright © 1991 by Marilyn Price.

Pages 100–101: ''Puppet Play'' by Marilyn Price. Copyright © 1991 by Marilyn Price.

Pages 102–103: ''The Engineer'' from *Now We Are Six* by A. A. Milne. Copyright 1927 by E. P. Dutton, renewed 1955 by A. A. Milne. Used by permission of Dutton Children's Books, a division of Penguin Books USA, Inc.

Pages 104–116: From *A Bicycle for Rosaura* by Daniel Barbot, illustrated by Morella Fuenmayor. Copyright © 1990 Ediciones Ekaré-Banco del Libro. Reprinted by permission of Kane/Miller Book Publishers.

Artists

Cathy Saksa, cover, 1–5, 117, 118–119, 120–121, 122, 128
Bernie Fuchs, 6–28
Kate Wolfe-Pagni, 6, 29
Aliki, 30–41, 120
Bill Peet, 42–79
Carolyn Croll, 80–99
Linda Kelen, 102–103
Morella Fuenmayor, 104–116

Photographs

Page 76: Courtesy of Bill Peet
Page 100: Courtesy of Marilyn Price
Page 122: Jeff Foott/Bruce Coleman, Inc.
Page 125, 127: Brown Brothers
Page 126: Gregg Mancuso/Stock Boston

Glossary

The contents of the Glossary have been adapted from *Beginning Dictionary*, Copyright © 1988, Scott, Foresman and Company.